# Why Am I Here?

JANET WESTADT

ISBN 979-8-88685-837-2 (paperback)
ISBN 979-8-88685-839-6 (digital)

Copyright © 2023 by Janet Westadt

All rights reserved. No part of this publication may be reproduced, distributed, or transmitted in any form or by any means, including photocopying, recording, or other electronic or mechanical methods without the prior written permission of the publisher. For permission requests, solicit the publisher via the address below.

Christian Faith Publishing
832 Park Avenue
Meadville, PA 16335
www.christianfaithpublishing.com

All biblical citations were taken from the New International Version of the Holy Bible unless otherwise indicated.

Printed in the United States of America

# CONTENTS

# ACKNOWLEDGMENTS

To God from whom all good things come.

To my husband, Dan, my soul mate. Thank you for your love, encouragement, and guidance.

To my children, Joe and Kim, you're the best.

To my beautiful grandchildren—Reagan, Keira, Samantha, Tenley, and Jaxon—you are God's greatest gifts.

To the rest of my family, thank you. Love you all.

I would like to acknowledge and thank these special people who helped me along my journey in getting this book to where it needs to be.

My pastors Dr. Trevon Gross and Pastor Qwynn Gross for all their wonderful teachings throughout the years, you are an inspiration, and thanks PT for taking the time to read through this and providing your feedback.

Janice Rodriques for the encouragement and for asking that important question: "So what are you doing today to move forward?"

Cathy Curran, I'm so glad God reunited us after all these years. His timing is perfect. I appreciate all your guidance.

Dan Westadt, Joe Moore, Linda Mills, and Valerie Penksa, thanks for reading and providing your valuable feedback.

# INTRODUCTION

My granddaughters were staying with us for the weekend, which is always an adventure. We enjoy the time we get to spend with them, and they are always curious like most kids are, asking us all kinds of questions. Why does it rain so much? Who is that lady you said hi to? What are we doing when we get to your house? How come we can't go shopping today?

On Saturday afternoon, my oldest granddaughter asked me, "Grandma, who is God?"

I was fumbling with the answer and told her something like, "He's our Father in heaven who created everything." She seemed to be happy with that answer, but I wasn't. It made me realize that I wasn't prepared enough to give her the best answer that I could.

So that led me to start writing a children's book explaining who God is. It would also include answers to other questions that kids have related to Jesus, angels, etc.

However, once I started writing, it dawned on me that I have heard countless people saying things like, "If there is a God, how can he let this happen, or why am I here, or what can I do?"

This made me realize that they are also searching for answers but don't know how or where to find them. It made me change my focus, from children to adults. How can adults help children understand if they don't know themselves? It's like when you are on an airplane and the flight attendant explains how you should put your mask on first before helping your child put on theirs.

It is the adults that need the answers. They need to know about God, his purpose for our lives, and how he wants us to come to him like children.

"Jesus said, 'Let the little children come to me, and do not hinder them, for the kingdom of heaven belongs to such as these'" (Matthew 19:14).

This is my attempt at answering those difficult questions people have. This is my Christian apologetic or, as my sister so cleverly stated, the answers according to Janet. The answers are Bible based but will have my take on why I believe them to be true.

Why the Bible? Because I believe it to be God's written Word. I hope and pray that once you read through this book, you will believe it too.

I have included Bible scriptures for reference. The reference starts with the name of the book then the number of the chapter and verse(s).

The Bible, for those who are not familiar with it, was written by man but inspired by God. It is a set of books that are split into two parts: the Old and the New Testaments. For the Christian, the Old Testament became history when Jesus Christ was born. "The disciples were called Christians first at Antioch" (Acts 11:26). His birth, death, and resurrection fulfilled the prophesy contained in the Old Testament.

The New Testament details Jesus's life on earth and explains how we can obtain eternal life. It ends with the book of Revelation when the angel of God reveals to John what will happen at the end of times when Jesus comes again.

"Look, I am coming soon! Blessed is the one who keeps the words of the prophecy written in this scroll" (Revelation 22:7).

God is the answer to everything. I am not talking about religion but life itself. If you want to live the best life you could ever possibly have here on earth, then it starts with believing in God. When you do that and follow him, you don't ever have to worry about what will happen to you and especially when your time here on earth is over.

Here is an off-the-wall example that shows why I believe the Bible has the answer to everything we, as God's people, need to know.

My sister and sister-in-law decided to stop coloring their hair and go "natural." They asked me what I thought and would I want to join them. I was really on the fence about it. I didn't like the idea of looking like "an old lady" especially since I didn't feel old. I just couldn't understand why girls would actually choose to dye their hair either gray or white.

I remembered when my older cousin decided to do the same thing. I didn't like it and thought she looked so much better with her blond hair.

My mother, God rest her soul, continued to dye her hair black, her natural color, till her late seventies. I think that also influenced my reluctance to let go.

It just so happened that I was reading the book of Proverbs at the time, and there it was: "Gray hair is a crown of splendor; it is attained in the way of righteousness" (Proverbs 16:31).

This was more than just a coincidence. God knew I was struggling with this decision and showed me the correct path. After all, who could argue with that passage? Who doesn't want to be righteous?

So I decided to join the ladies of my family. The more I thought about it, the more I realized it was the right decision. Now I am saving money, time, and my body from all those unnecessary chemicals.

My real-life experiences are included in the "answers" to show why I believe as I do. I also have other examples that people have told me from their own situations. I challenge you to look at your own life to see if you might have experienced something similar.

My father served in the military when he was just seventeen years old. He lied about his age in order to join the army. During his time of service, he was one of the soldiers involved in the Allied invasion of Normandy during World War II.

He saw his buddy get his head blown off, which he only told me about once when he was in a very melancholy mood. I also found out that my dad was captured and became a POW, prisoner of war. He very rarely spoke about this time in his life.

He told me that the Germans hated the Americans because if it wasn't for us, they would have won the war. Because of this, the American soldiers were treated the worst. He didn't give details, but

I'm sure it's the reason he became an alcoholic. He had trouble handling the atrocities of war that he saw and experienced.

Life was not great growing up, but as an adult, I came to understand why my father was the way he was. He did his best to be a good parent. We never went hungry and always had a roof over our heads and clean clothes to wear. He tried to do the right things like taking us to church once in a while. We kids didn't like it because we didn't understand it.

The reason I bring this up is to show that not everyone is fortunate enough to grow up having the ideal family life. Life is not easy especially if you are trying to do it alone. There are difficult times, and sometimes, it's not easy to do the right things.

I am here to tell you that we are blessed because we don't have to be alone. We have a heavenly Father that wants to help us each and every day and that loves us so much that he sent his only Son to die for us so that we can be with him forever.

As a parent, I can tell you that it is not an easy job. We provide for our children, show them love, and try to raise them to be independent and able to take care of themselves in the best way possible.

But God wants to do more. Our heavenly Father wants us to be dependent on him. He tells us that he will provide for our needs.

"And my God will meet all your needs according to the riches of his glory in Christ Jesus" (Philippians 4:19).

Here's my disclaimer: I am not a Bible scholar and don't pretend to be.

I have attempted to answer these difficult questions by praying and using the New International Version of the Holy Bible as my source. Please take the time to read the scriptures yourself with whatever version you have, and most importantly, pray to God, and ask for clarity and understanding.

"Trust in the Lord with all your heart and lean not on your own understanding; in all your ways submit to him, and he will make your paths straight" (Proverbs 3:5–6).

I hope this book and the answers they contain help you in your life's journey. Because our time here is limited, it's critical for me to share the good news with God's people, you. Once the seed is planted, that's when God takes over.

God wants all his people to be with him in eternity.

Agape, Janet.

# CHAPTER 1

# Is There a God?

*Whoever does not love does not know God, because God is love.*

—1 John 4:8

When you look at the headlines in the newspaper, online newsfeed, or TV news headlines, what do you see? The news is covered with shootings, rioting, looting, and violence by all types and ages of people. It's no wonder people doubt the existence of God.

Our country has seen horrific crimes committed against our children with school shootings and sexual mistreatments. We ask, "God, where were you?"

Schools in the past have been a safe haven. We would drop our children off at school in the morning with confidence, knowing they would be cared for in a place of learning. What are they learning now?

Schools have locked doors and metal detectors. Teachers are being trained to use handguns. Police are on the ready in case of some type of attack.

God was taken out of our public schools when school prayer was abolished in 1962 and then the Bible was removed in 1963. No longer was a school day opened with prayer. No longer did teachers thank God for the day and ask for guidance and protection for everyone. Instead, the door became open for Satan and evil.

These heinous crimes are committed by people filled with hate, not love. When people grow up with hate, it is difficult to know God because they do not know about love. I've heard it said and believe it to be true: "Hurting people hurt people."

My daughter went to Virginia Tech and lived in the dorm where a shooting occurred. Thank God it was several years before that happened. My stepson went to Northern Illinois where there was a shooting. The college I attended also had a drive-by shooting a couple of days after I was on campus.

People we trust with our children, to teach them and nurture them, take advantage of their innocence. They are told lies and are manipulated by people filled with evil intent. Yes, even religious leaders commit heinous crimes. These evildoers will eventually be punished. But we, as parents, need to do more.

We need to start the day with God by praying over our children before we send them out into the world. Prayer is a powerful tool we have available to us. You'll see other examples of how my prayers have been answered in a later chapter.

My husband, Dan, told me that after his first son was born and the first time he held him, he had an epiphany. He could see the beauty of God's creation in the face of his newborn baby. It was the miracle of life. From then on, he had no doubt of God's existence.

This is love. This is God.

I know there must be a being, something greater than myself. I feel it and can't deny it. But how do I know it's God? When I take a walk outside and see the trees, hear the birds, and look at all the flowers, I know there must have been a master plan.

Something this wonderful did not just happen. Everything works together as it should. It had to have been created by an intelligent, all-knowing being. I don't believe it just happened. It's too complex for that.

Like my husband, when I look at my children and my grandchildren, I can't help but see them as a miracle, a blessing from God. People, animals, and all creatures are designed so uniquely. They all have a purpose even though we may not know what it is.

For example, I still don't understand why there are rats in this world or cockroaches. But in the grand scheme of things, I don't really need to know. All I need to know is how to avoid them.

Why is it that we can believe in someone having an intuition about something, a sixth sense, a gut feeling but have trouble believing there is a loving being called God that is directing our steps if we only listen? Why can we have dumb luck, be lucky, be in the right place at the right time but not know this was set up for us by a God who loves us and cares about us?

When I pray, my prayers are not only answered but also with the best possible solution. It's always better than I could have imagined. When he could have provided two extra tickets, I got four together instead. You'll see this in a later chapter.

There is an intelligent being that communicates to us and wants us to communicate back. I find it difficult to not believe there is a God especially when I read the Bible, God's Word. This book has it all, all the instructions we need to live the best possible life here on earth. It also tells us what will happen at the end. I can follow this book and know things will work out for me, for my life and my death.

God said that he was the Alpha and the Omega, the beginning and the end. When I take the time to really think about this statement, I can't find any reason, no logical explanation that tells me this is wrong.

What you believe is a choice. I made an active decision and chose to believe in God. It wasn't easy. I faced opposition, but I also found peace. I no longer had to face living this existence alone. Plus I had clear instructions as to how to live this life. I'm a person that likes things spelled out, so for me, there was no other way. Jesus is the way.

God gave us free will because he wanted us to decide for ourselves. This is our choice. He wants us to come to him freely. If you believe that there is a supreme being, why not believe it is God? What is stopping you?

It makes me wonder, why do people when they are desperate or when they see no other options cry out to God? If you don't believe in him or believe he exists, what is the reason? I believe it is because it is our spirit that is calling out.

God created the world, and he created man and woman in his own image. It is not our physical being, the one that we see in the mirror, but his image, that of a spirit.

We are all spirits with a soul (our inner being—who we are on the inside) that are born on this earth into a body. It has been proven by the medical profession that at the time of our death, our body weighs less. This is due to our soul (and spirit) leaving the body.

God created the spirit/soul of Adam and Eve. Then he created them as physical beings, Adam from dust and Eve from Adam's rib. God was present with them in the Garden of Eden. They walked with God and talked with him. They lived in total freedom. They were given access to everything the world had to offer. They were without sin and enjoyed life as God intended, walking side by side.

There was only one exception. They were not to eat the fruit of the tree of the knowledge of good and evil. The temptation was too great, and Eve is tricked into eating the forbidden fruit and sharing it with Adam.

Their eyes were opened. They went from only knowing God's love and goodness and having eternal life with God to knowing evil and no longer being able to be in the physical presence of God.

Because of their disobedience (sin against God) of eating from that tree, they are banished from the garden, and their (man's) relationship with God changes.

So they were now separated from God, kicked out of paradise where all their needs were met, and no longer have eternal life. God told Adam that it was because of him that the ground was now cursed, and he would have to work the land for food all the days of his life.

This is true today. If you don't work, you don't eat.

God told the woman that he will make childbearing very severe with painful labor.

Being a mother and giving birth twice, I can attest to what was written in the Bible about childbearing and labor as 100 percent true. Not only does your body change as you are carrying a child but also after.

My fingers and toes swelled. My breasts grew. My stomach bulged, and my feet grew from a shoe size of seven and a half to an eight and a half. I developed gallstones after my first child and had to have surgery to have my gallbladder removed.

Labor can last for hours with contractions coming and going until the time when your baby is finally delivered. It's not fun, but at least, there is a reward when it is over.

God also said that her desire would be for her husband and that he would rule over her. Here again, God's statement to the woman is 100 percent true. When you agree to get married, the two are joined as one, and the woman usually takes the man's last name. If this does not happen, the children still assume the father's last name.

Men are the ones who "rule" this world, and women, in a lot of countries, are still considered second-class citizens. Can you imagine if all men were to follow God and lead as they should, how much better the world would be? Filled with love: love of God, love of family, love for your neighbor.

I have a hard time trying to disprove that there is a God when I read words in the very first book of the Bible and know them to be true from my own experience.

Because of his great love for us, every one of us with no exception, God wants to restore our relationship with him. However, he cannot tolerate sin, and the sin must be cleansed before that can happen. The Old Testament speaks about the temporary fix, which was for man to make an animal sacrifice.

Also in the Old Testament are scriptures that foretell Jesus's coming. He is the ultimate sacrifice, the sacrificial lamb.

"Therefore the Lord himself will give you a sign: The virgin will conceive and give birth to a son and will call him Immanuel" (Isaiah 7:14).

Immanuel means *God with us.*

"For God so loved the world that he gave his one and only Son, that whoever believes in him shall not perish but have eternal life" (John 3:16)

God sends his Son, Jesus, to be the savior of mankind. Who would do that? And why?

> This is how God showed his love among us: He sent his one and only Son into the world that we might live through him. This is love: not that we loved God, but that he loved us and sent his Son as an atoning sacrifice for our sins. Dear friends, since God so loved us, we also ought to love one another. No one has ever seen God; but if we love one another, God lives in us and his love is made complete in us. (1 John 4:9–12)

Yes, there is a God, and he is love, and he loves you. If you know love, know that there is a God. If you don't know love, know this: No one else would ever give up their only son to die a painful death for someone that hates them, condemns them, or doesn't acknowledge them and what they've done for them. No one else would want to spend eternity with someone who would do those things. This is love.

God exists as Godhead, one God in three persons: Father, Son (Jesus), and Holy Ghost (or Spirit). God the Father is the creator of all.

"I am the Alpha and the Omega," says the Lord God, "who is, and who was, and who is to come, the Almighty" (Revelation 1:8).

"Turn to me and be saved, all you ends of the earth; for I am God, and there is no other" (Isaiah 45:22).

Jesus is our Savior, and only through him can we have eternal life with God.

"No one has ever seen God, but the one and only Son, who is himself God and is in closest relationship with the Father, has made him known" (John 1:18).

In the New Testament, an angel of the Lord visited Joseph, Mary's husband, in a dream after he found out that she was pregnant. The angel told Joseph the following:

> Joseph son of David, do not be afraid to take Mary home as your wife, because what is conceived in her is from the Holy Spirit. She will

> give birth to a son, and you are to give him the
> name Jesus, because he will save his people from
> their sins. (Matthew 1:20–21)

We know that Jesus did live on this earth, and it was recorded in the census that was taken back in that time. The census is still performed today.

When Jesus asks Peter who he thought Jesus was, this was his response: "Peter answered, 'God's Messiah'" (Luke 9:20).

Messiah is the anointed one, the savior of a group of people.

When asked about being the Messiah, Jesus declares, "I and the Father are one" (John 10:30).

> Thomas said to him, "Lord, we don't know
> where you are going, so how can we know the
> way?" Jesus answered, "I am the way and the
> truth and the life. No one comes to the Father
> except through me." (John 14:5–6)

When Jesus was baptized by John, we get confirmation of who Jesus is. As Jesus comes out of the water, heaven opens, and the Spirit of God, like a dove, descends on him. Then a voice is heard claiming, "This is my Son, whom I love; with him I am well pleased," which can be found in Matthew 3:16–17.

The Holy Spirit is the third part of the Godhead. The Holy Spirit is our guide through this life on earth.

As you can see by the two scriptures below, Jesus wants his followers to know that the Holy Spirit is the Spirit of truth and comes from the Father in the name of the Son. We are given a guide to help us navigate this life on earth.

"But the Advocate, the Holy Spirit, whom the Father will send in my name, will teach you all things and will remind you of everything I have said to you" (John 14:26).

"When the Advocate comes, whom I will send to you from the Father-the Spirit of truth who goes out from the Father-he will testify about me" (John 15:26).

Each part of the Godhead is to be worshipped for who they are and what they do.

"In the beginning God created the heavens and the earth" (Genesis 1:1).

If you continue reading Genesis, you will find that God the Father created everything in six days and rested on the seventh.

"Then God blessed the seventh day and made it holy, because on it he rested from all the work of creating that he had done" (Genesis 2:3).

We honor God on Sunday by going to church to give him thanks and praise and by resting from work. This is a day meant to celebrate his goodness and spend time with family and friends. All good things come from God.

Who hasn't seen those signs? *John 3:16.*

I know I have seen them everywhere: on the roadside, at sporting events, anywhere large crowds of people may be gathered. People who take the time to write the signs and hold them up are doing God's work, spreading the good news of Jesus.

What does it mean? It means that we can now have eternal life with God if we believe. Our body will die, but our spirit will live on with God.

Who is it meant for? Everyone with no exception. But you have to believe.

Jesus is the good news. It's the real reason we celebrate Christmas, the birth of Christ. It's only a shopping frenzy if you make it that way. Stop, and take the time to enjoy the season. Let's remember that we give gifts as the three wise men did as a celebration of God's gift to his people, his Son.

I remember my former brother-in-law saying that his favorite holiday was Thanksgiving. He always felt that Christmas was too commercial and that people lost its true meaning.

> But the angel said to them, "Do not be
> afraid. I bring you good news that will cause
> great joy for all the people. Today in the town

of David a Savior has been born to you; he is the
Messiah, the Lord." (Luke 2:10–11)

When Jesus was crucified, his shed blood is what makes mankind pure again and wipes away the sin that was created from the disobedience of Adam and Eve and all sin that follows. Jesus's sacrifice—becoming man, shedding his blood, dying on the cross, and then being resurrected (coming back to life)—restores mankind's relationship with God.

> Once you were alienated from God and were enemies in your minds because of your evil behavior. But now he has reconciled you by Christ's physical body through death to present you holy in his sight, without blemish and free from accusation-if you continue in your faith, established and firm, and do not move from the hope held out in the gospel. This is the gospel that you heard and that has been proclaimed to every creature under heaven, and of which, I, Paul have become a servant. (Colossians 1:21–23)

Jesus's crucifixion and resurrection are the reason we celebrate Easter. Our Savior has risen from the dead.

Jesus meets with the apostles. He knows that they will have struggles in this world and will need help. The apostles receive the gift of the Holy Spirit, the Advocate.

> When the day of Pentecost came, they were all together in one place. Suddenly a sound like the blowing of a violent wind came from heaven and filled the whole house where they were sitting. They saw what seemed to be tongues of fire that separated and came to rest on each of them. All of them were filled with the Holy Spirit

and began to speak in other tongues as the Spirit
enabled them. (Acts 2:1–4)

"This is how we know that we live in him and he in us: He has given us of his Spirit" (1 John 4:13).

Let's look at this physical example of God's presence that can be seen today. The background can be found in the story of Noah and the Ark from the book of Genesis.

God was not happy with mankind and their wickedness, but God found Noah to be a righteous man. He decided to send a great flood to destroy all creatures on the earth and tells Noah to build an ark for him and his family and include two of each creature (male and female). The ark saved them from the flood, and to give thanks, Noah built an altar to the Lord and sacrificed burnt offerings on it.

When God smelled the aroma, he decided that he would never again destroy all living creatures, "even though every inclination of the human heart is evil from childhood" (Genesis 8:21), and made a covenant with Noah and all generations to come.

"I have set my rainbow in the clouds, and it will be the sign of the covenant between me and the earth" (Genesis 9:13).

"Whenever the rainbow appears in the clouds, I will see it and remember the everlasting covenant between God and all living creatures of every kind on the earth" (Genesis 9:16).

Before the flood and before God established this covenant, there was no rainbow. After the forty days of rain when Noah opened a window and sent a raven out, he did not see a rainbow.

So the next time you see a rainbow in the sky, know that God exists. He sees the rainbow too and remembers his promise.

A rainbow is a symbol of God's promise to everyone, but unfortunately, most people only see it as a symbol of the LGBTQ+ community.

Statistics show that there are 2.38 billion Christians in the world. That is one-third of the world's population.

There are 1.8 billion Muslims who also believe in the existence of God, Allah, which is nearly one-fourth of the world's population.

The Jewish population who follow Yahweh (God) totals about 15.2 million.

So here is a question for you: why do so many people believe in the existence of God?

"You believe that there is one God. Good! Even the demons believe that-and shudder" (James 2:19).

# CHAPTER 2

# How Do I Know I Am Hearing from God?

*Whoever belongs to God hears what God says. The reason you do not hear is that you do not belong to God.*

—John 8:47

God speaks to us in many different ways: through his angels, in dreams, in promptings, through people with specific physical signs.

"When the angel of the Lord appeared to Gideon, he said, 'The Lord is with you, mighty warrior'" (Judges 6:12).

How do I know that the message I'm receiving is truly from God? In order to know if it's from God and not from someone else, like Satan or even ourselves, you have to put it to the test.

Is it something for my good or the good of someone else? God will never tell you to do something that will hurt you or anyone else. Is it something you would normally do, or is it out of the ordinary?

There are times I get promptings, a feeling such as giving the guy pumping my gas a little money (I live in New Jersey, and we are not allowed to pump our own gas) or buying some donuts for the car shop working on my car.

It's a small gesture, but I don't know if that person could use a little something to brighten their day. Maybe they didn't get a chance to eat breakfast that day before going to work, or maybe they got a bill they didn't expect and could use a few dollars to tide them over.

God works through people, so if you receive some type of message like that, follow it. God is using you, and you never know what that small gesture can do for a person. It may be small, but it is a way to show love. We need more love in this world.

I was leaving the parking lot of a local store and saw a woman holding a baby and a young girl that was with her. I could see that she was very sad, and the girl was holding up a sign asking for money. I drove slowly past them but felt a pull to turn around and go back.

I got out some money from my purse and gave it to the girl. She smiled, and I drove off. Yes, they could have been scamming me, or they could be in dire need. I will never know, but God knows. That's what counts.

"Give to everyone who asks you, and if anyone takes what belongs to you, do not demand it back. Do to others as you would have them do to you" (Luke 6:30–31).

The more good we do for others, the better place this world will be. It's like a snowball effect. It continues to grow from a little goodwill gesture.

Did you receive some type of confirmation? It could be a sign or someone confirming what you have been asking about. This could happen even if you didn't ask for it.

While my husband, Dan, and I were still dating and we were both living in Virginia, he made plans to move to Illinois for a new job opportunity. The night before he was going to drive out to the Midwest and start a new life, I was helping clean his apartment and finishing up packing the U-Haul he was going to drive out there.

It was a very difficult time because we had gotten close, and I didn't know what would happen with our relationship. Dan told me later on that he had no doubts we were going to be together forever, no matter where we were located.

Once we were done, we decided to get something to eat, so we drove to the local Subway. There were no parking places in front of the store, so we had to park further down the road. Dan said that he would go in, so I told him what I wanted, and he got out of the car.

During that time, I was in tears and started to pray asking God for some type of sign that this would not be the end of our relationship and that Dan and I were meant to be together. Was he my soul mate, and were we supposed to be together? That's when I looked up and saw where we were parked, in front of the store called "Sole Mates."

We've been married for twenty-two years. There's my sign.

When my daughter found out she was expecting twins, she asked me when I was moving back to New Jersey, my home state and where she was located. I knew how important it was, so Dan and I decided that I would move back while he stayed behind to sell our house in Illinois. We were attending a church in Arlington Heights, Illinois, at the time.

At the end of the last service we attended together, the pastor hurried over to us, and as he shook hands with Dan, he said, "You can come by yourself!"

I had never seen the pastor do that before. It was always his wife that greeted everyone as they left. It also struck me as an odd thing to say. He had no idea of the plans we had made.

Later, Dan told me that he was thinking during the service if he should attend Lakewood Chapel without me. We both realized God gave him confirmation, through the Pastor, that this was exactly what he was supposed to do.

I attended our annual women's conference on Friday and Saturday. One of the speakers stayed an extra day and spoke during our church's Sunday services. Our guest pastor opens herself up and lets the Holy Spirit speak through her. She spoke and prayed over people within the services.

I attended the first service and saw her pray over a man that had recently overcome cancer. She had no idea who the man was and what he had gone through, but the Holy Spirit told him God knew what he went through and was with him. I can't remember all the details, but I know this man was given a special message.

After service was over, I drove home. Our church does a livestream, so I hooked up my computer to the TV and was able to see part of the second service. As I watched, I asked God if he would speak to my son through this guest pastor. I knew he was attending this service because I saw him drive into the parking lot as I was leaving. She spoke to several people but not Joe. Then the online feed cut off.

My husband plays in the church band and after the second service sent a picture to me through his phone. It was a picture of my son with the guest pastor praying over him. I thanked him for sending me confirmation that my prayer had been answered.

Another way you can confirm if the message is from God is to ask yourself if there is a biblical reference. Can you find it in the scriptures? We are fortunate that a quick Google search can usually bring up Scripture passages related to the answer we are looking for.

> Now the Berean Jews were of more noble character than those in Thessalonica, for they received the message with great eagerness and examined the Scriptures every day to see if what Paul said was true. (Acts 17:11)

As I mentioned in my introduction, God confirmed, through his Word, that letting my hair go gray was what I was supposed to do.

As I have been putting together this book, I have been praying for God's help and guidance. It seems like every morning, I have received messages on what to include, how to explain certain things, and what experiences I should share. This is the Holy Spirit speaking to me in the quiet of my mind.

In the past couple of weeks, as this book has been going through the editing stages, I have been constantly reminded of a near-tragic incident that God prevented me from making and that I have never told anyone about. I believe God wanted me to include it in this book to show that he is not only protecting us from our own stupidity but the ones closest to us.

There was a seafood restaurant that members of my family enjoyed going to. You had to take this small bridge to get to it since it is on the water. We decided, after drinking for a while, that we were hungry and wanted to get something to eat. So we hopped into my car and started driving. When I got to the bridge, it was blocked off, and I remember thinking, *That's not right.* So I drove around the barrier.

At just the right time, I got this feeling to stop the car. I can't even remember who was in the car at the time and if they realized what happened. When I looked out from the dashboard, I saw why there was a barrier. The rest of the bridge was completely gone. I would have driven us over the edge of the bridge.

This happened over fifty years ago, and I still thank God for his goodness.

My husband and I have been able to retire from our full-time jobs. With collecting social security, having a 401(k), and making some other major decisions, we know we will be comfortable, financially, for the rest of our lives.

Well, during the past several months, I have been contacted by a company to do some outside consulting. I wasn't sure about taking the job but decided to give it a try since it is part-time. Hours are flexible, and I am working from home. It can't get any better than that!

When I attended my first staff meeting, they opened with prayer. Come to find out the owners are Christians. God gave me confirmation that this opportunity came from him, and I made the right decision in taking the job.

I had been praying for God to help me become more of a blessing to others. He answered my prayers with this job opportunity. With the extra money I will make, I can be more generous toward others.

God is always speaking to us, and we need to get better at listening. Go somewhere quiet. Pray and meditate on God's Word, the Bible. Read a scripture, and really think about what it says. Is there a message for you in it?

It's during those times when we get closer to him that we will be more open to hearing his voice.

"For no word from God will ever fail" (Luke 1:37).

# CHAPTER 3

## Is There a Heaven and a Hell?

*In the beginning God created the heavens and the earth.*

—Genesis 1:1

When people think of heaven, they usually picture clouds with the sunlight streaking through and angels playing harps. This is what is depicted in quite a few pieces of artwork I have seen in museums.

Have you ever been to a place that was idyllic? I was fortunate enough to visit Hawaii on a two-week vacation through the generosity of my good friend and a couple she is close to. I know that God works through people, and I think this was part of God's plan to bless me. He gave me the opportunity to see what heaven would be like for me.

Our first week was in Kauai, nicknamed the Garden Island. We walked along the beaches, were entertained by whales, saw sea turtles swimming by the rocks, took ukulele lessons, and swam. I don't remember ever being this relaxed in my entire life.

On Kauai, there are chicken roaming freely all over the island. We saw them on the beach and in the parking lot of the local shopping mall where we got massages, an indulgence I enjoy whenever I can.

Like Indiana Jones, I too fear snakes. They are not native to Hawaii, which gave me another reason to feel like I was in paradise.

Our second week was in Maui, a more touristy place. We went to a luau and shopped for souvenirs. I even bought a couple of ukuleles, one for me and one for my husband. What better way to relax than to strum a uke while enjoying a beautiful sunset?

The food was so good! For breakfast, I discovered coconut syrup, which was even better than maple syrup on pancakes. We ate fresh seafood, and I enjoyed my favorite fruit, pineapple. I had it in a drink that the kids like called POG, a combination of pineapple, orange, and guava juice, and found a bottle of pineapple wine.

The best part of the vacation in Hawaii was the sunshine and tropical weather. It rained daily, but it was like a light sun-shower and brought the most beautiful rainbows. I even saw a double rainbow, something I had never seen before. I was in awe.

And the flowers were as big as my head and bursting with all different colors. It was a feast for the eyes.

God created Hawaii, and I was able to see and experience it. If he can create a place like this, that I was able to see and enjoy, then I have to believe there is a heaven, which has to be even more beautiful.

We do know some things about heaven from reading the Bible. God created heaven, and it is his throne. It is also where Jesus is seated, at our Father's right hand. The only way to heaven is through Jesus, our Savior who takes away our sins.

"But I tell you, do not swear an oath at all: either by heaven, for it is God's throne; or by the earth, for it is his footstool;…" (Matthew 5:34–35).

Do I know 100 percent that there is a heaven? Yes, I know it through having faith in God. I know it by reading the Bible, his Word. I know that I was created as a spirit before I even had a body, and when this body dies, I know my spirit will be going someplace. I want it to go where my God resides, in heaven. It's his plan that all his people are with him because he loves us.

When my sister was in her early twenties and living at home, there was a day when she was feeling faint. She went into the bathroom to splash some water on her face. She said that she knows she wasn't eating right and maybe just had a cup of coffee that morning.

She passed out and remembers feeling a sense of euphoria, happiness, and joy like she had never felt before. She had no feeling of physical form, and it was dark, but she saw little lights, not like candles, but felt the presence of other beings, good and welcoming. She kept wondering, *Where am I? What is going on? And maybe this is what death is.*

During this time, her boyfriend and I got the bathroom door open, and it looked like she was having convulsions or some type of seizure. We kept trying to wake her up. She told us that if we weren't there, she would not have come back. She said that she has no fear of death now.

"To the Lord your God belong the heavens, even the highest heavens the earth and everything in it" (Deuteronomy 10:14).

I suggest you watch a couple of YouTube videos with testimonies of people who have had near-death experiences and claim they have seen heaven. Listen to how they felt and how they now live their lives.

Yes, I believe there is a heaven and that there is a hell. Hell is separation from God, from all that is good.

When my son was younger and playing peewee football, his team was supposed to go on a bus to the game as it was a distance away. I had to work, so his father dropped him off. I asked him to follow the bus, but he didn't wait and drove to the game location instead. This was the time before everyone had cell phones.

When I came home from work, I found out that the game had been canceled and the bus never left. His father drove back to the place where the bus was leaving from, but no one was there. We had no idea where my son was at. During that time, I was going through hell, separation from my son.

Turns out one of his coaches took him home with him and his son. They had waited for a while for someone to pick him up but then decided to leave. We got a phone call later that day. Thank God he was safe.

As I am writing this book, Ukraine is being attacked by Russia. Children are being killed; it seems that humanity is gone. So parents are sending their own children to other countries as refugees in order to keep them safe. It is a heartbreaking situation. I pray the people in those countries take care of these children like that coach took care of my son.

The Ukrainians are living through their own hell right now. I cannot imagine how they must feel being separated from their children and not knowing how or where they are. I can only hope their faith in God will help them get through the evil they are facing.

We wonder how this could be happening, but the Bible tells us in Ephesians 6:12 that our struggle is not against flesh and blood but against spiritual forces of evil in high places. Just as God works through people, so does the enemy. That is the only explanation for the actions of the Russian president. He is not filled with love but hate, and hate comes from the enemy.

Hell is also a place—Hades, devoid of love, a place of pain and suffering.

The Gospels of Matthew, Mark, and Luke give you an idea of what it is like and who will be there.

"Not everyone who says to me, 'Lord, Lord,' will enter the kingdom of heaven, but only the one who does the will of my Father who is in heaven" (Matthew 7:21).

"And you, Capernaum, will you be lifted to the heavens? No, you will go down to Hades" (Matthew 11:23).

"And if your eye causes you to stumble, gouge it out and throw it away. It is better for you to enter life with one eye than to have two eyes and be thrown into the fire of hell" (Matthew 18:9).

"You snakes! You brood of vipers! How will you escape being condemned to hell?" (Matthew 23:33).

In the book of Luke, Chapter 16, we see what happened to a rich man and a beggar named Lazarus after they had both died. The rich man ended up in Hades, in torment. He looked up and could see Abraham with Lazarus by his side. He cried out for Lazarus to dip the tip of his finger in water and bring it to him so his tongue could be cooled because he was in agony from the fire.

Abraham's response is that during his lifetime, the rich man received good things, while Lazarus did not. Now Lazarus is being comforted, and he is in agony. He also says, "there is a 'chasm' that was set in place so you cannot cross over between the two places."

If the rich man had helped Lazarus while they were still alive, things would have been different for him.

"A generous person will prosper; whoever refreshes others will be refreshed" (Proverbs 11:25).

Have you heard the saying "hell on earth"? Maybe you are living it right now. If you are in a bad situation, check your relationship with God. Is God a part of your life? You don't have to be alone to deal with your situation. Ask God to come into your life. He can handle it for you. He can help you through it.

> And I tell you that you are Peter, and on this rock I will build my church, and the gates of Hades will not overcome it. I will give you the keys of the kingdom of heaven, and whatever you bind on earth will be bound in heaven, and whatever you loose on earth will be loosed in heaven. (Matthew 16:18)

"But I will show you whom you should fear: Fear him who, after your body has been killed, has authority to throw you into hell. Yes, I tell you, fear him" (Luke 12:5).

Be careful how you live your life here on earth. We are not here forever, only temporarily. How you live now will determine where you end up.

> The acts of the flesh are obvious: sexual immorality, impurity and debauchery; idolatry and witchcraft; hatred, discord, jealousy, fits of rage, selfish ambition, dissensions, factions and envy; drunkenness, orgies, and the like. I warn you, as I did before, that those who live like this will not inherit the kingdom of God. (Galatians 5:19–21)

Again, I suggest you watch a couple of YouTube videos with testimonies of people who have had near-death experiences especially the ones that say they saw hell. Take it as their warning to you. They are turning their lives around because of what they experienced and don't want to end up there.

The worst thing you could say to someone is, "Go to hell." I wouldn't wish that on anyone.

God also promises us a new heaven if we remain faithful to him. I plan on being there and pray you will be too.

"See, I will create new heavens and a new earth. The former things will not be remembered, nor will they come to mind" (Isaiah 65:17).

"Then I saw 'a new heaven and a new earth,' for the first heaven and the first earth has passed away, and there was no longer any sea" (Revelation 21:1).

# CHAPTER 4

## Are Angels Real?

*In speaking of the angels he says, "He makes his angels spirits, and his servants flames of fire."*

—Hebrews 1:7

Angels are spirits created by God, and their numbers are great. Although angels were created as higher beings, they are here to help mankind.

"Then I looked and heard the voice of many angels, numbering thousands upon thousands, and ten thousand times ten thousand…" (Revelation 5:11).

"Are not all angels ministering spirits sent to serve those who will inherit salvation?" (Hebrews 1:14).

Yes, angels are real and perform many tasks for God. One of those things is protecting us humans especially from ourselves and our bad choices.

When my husband was previously married, his family went on many camping trips. His oldest son was always very curious and often did things considered risky. On one particular trip when he was around six years old, he wandered off from the campsite, while his parents were busy setting up. He ended up falling off a cliff. Fortunately, he ended up having only minor injuries. He later told his mom and dad that the angel caught him while he was falling.

When my sister, brother, and I were growing up, we didn't have the ideal family situation. My mother ended up moving out, leaving us with an alcoholic dad. It was not easy, and each of us had our own battles fighting addiction as we got older.

When my brother was in the army, he told me about a time he was with a group of soldiers who were waiting to be deployed some- where. One of the guys approached him and asked if he wanted to go get high, and if so, meet him in the woods further out.

As he thought about it, another man approached him and asked him, "Why do you want to go with that guy? It might not be a good idea."

Fortunately, he realized that it was a bad idea and decided to stay where he was. When he turned to thank the man, he couldn't find him anywhere. He told me that somehow, he knew that this was not a man but was an angel sent to protect him.

I had a drinking problem when I was in my early twenties. I was working at the post office, and a couple of the guys would meet at the bar after work. I would meet them there every so often.

When it was near Christmastime, I remember stopping for a few. I left after a while and went to pick up my girlfriend since we were going to go out that night. On the way to her house, I blacked out and ended up totaling my car when I hit a tree. I had no idea what happened, but when I came to, a man came up to my window and asked if I was okay. I said, "Yes."

The street I was driving on was a very dark and lonely road. From what I remember, it was not the kind of street where someone would be going for a walk especially at night.

The man then asked me, "Was there an animal in the road, and did you swerve to avoid hitting it?"

I said, "Yes, that's what must have happened."

At the time, I wasn't sure if that was true, but this explana- tion kept me from getting into trouble, like being arrested for drunk driving.

The next thing I know, the people that lived in the house had called the police, and I was being helped out of the car. When the police asked me what happened, I told them I swerved to avoid hitting an animal on the road.

They asked me if I wanted to go to the hospital, and I said, "Yes." I remembered that if you said that, they couldn't give you a sobriety test, which I knew I wouldn't pass.

The car was towed to a gas station that was close by. When I was able to go see my car days later, I saw what a mess it was. I still had Christmas presents in the truck, which I was able to retrieve.

I thank God that no one was hurt by my accident. I know that he sent his angel to help me out of a very bad situation. I'm sure that angel directed my car into that tree rather than the house.

Be on your guard because angels can appear as normal men and as my brother, and I can attest.

"Do not forget to show hospitality to strangers, for by so doing some people have shown hospitality to angels without knowing it" (Hebrews 13:2).

Angels act as messengers for God. This is what happened to Zechariah. He was visited by the angel Gabriel who told him the news that his wife, Elizabeth, was going to bear him a son.

"The angel said to him, I am Gabriel. I stand in the presence of God, and I have been sent to speak to you and to tell you this good news" (Luke 1:19).

Angels are warriors and are at work around us though we can't see them.

When the servant of Elisha got up early in the morning and saw an army with horses and chariots had surrounded the city, he was worried. Elisha was not. In 2 Kings 6:17, we see that Elisha prayed and asked the Lord to open the servant's eyes so that he could see what Elisha saw, hills full of horses and chariots of fire.

The book of Joshua, Chapter 5, says that when he was near Jericho, he saw a man standing with a drawn sword. When he asked the man if he was for them or for their enemies, he responded back that it was neither and that he was the commander of the army of the Lord and has now come.

"Do you think I cannot call on my Father, and he will at once put at my disposal more than twelve legions of angels?" (Matthew 26:53).

Angels were there in the beginning when God created the heavens before man was created and will be there at the end of the world.

"The Son of Man will send out his angels, and they will weed out of his kingdom everything that causes sin and all who do evil" (Matthew 13:41).

Then I heard a loud voice from the temple saying to the seven angels, "Go pour out the seven bowls of God's wrath on the earth" (Revelation 16:1).

Have you ever been in a situation and something happened to keep you from getting harmed? You could have encountered an angel or angels.

I remember leaving a bar at one time after having a few drinks and driving on a major highway. I was driving erratically because I was upset about something, and I don't really remember why. All of a sudden, I got stuck in back of a large semi and saw another one position itself right in back of me. These drivers boxed me in so that I was forced to slow down and drive straight.

I worked with two women who died from driving drunk. You would think I would have known better. Were these God's angels protecting me from myself? I believe these truck drivers were.

Have you ever met a stranger who said something to you that you needed to hear and felt no fear? You could have encountered an angel.

But beware. There are also fallen angels, and Satan is their leader. They were thrown out of heaven and no longer serve God. How can we tell the difference? God is good. Satan is evil. You will know by their actions.

# CHAPTER 5

## Why Am I here?

*So God created mankind in his own image, in the image of
God he created them; male and female he created them.*

—Genesis 1:27

There was a time when I wondered the same thing: why am I here? As a child, I went to school, listened to my mom and dad, played, and did homework. As I grew up, I learned how to drive a car, worked several different jobs, and eventually moved out and had my own place. But I always felt that there had to be something more to life than just living day-to-day.

Growing up in an alcoholic home then marrying an alcoholic created so much drama that wasn't necessary. It seemed that everything was a big deal, and every occurrence was something to yell and complain about. It's very stressful!

At the suggestion of my parish priest, I started to attend Al-Anon meetings, the organization that helps families deal with alcoholism and the alcoholic in their lives. There, I learned how to cope with these stressful situations in a rational way.

This support group helped me change my way of thinking. I found that I cannot change someone else's behavior, only mine. I am responsible for my own self, not someone else. It is their choice to drink, and it has nothing to do with me.

They stress that we should rely on our "higher power" or a power greater than ourselves. I found this to be God, and here's why.

For those that are not familiar with this group, it is anonymous, and you only use first names. There are groups that meet at all different locations, at different times, and at different days/nights of the week.

I attended several different meetings, and each one had a uniqueness about it. That's because there are different people who run each meeting, although sometimes, you might run into someone from another meeting that you might have seen before.

I did see someone I knew from high school, and what struck me is that we were both dealing with the same type of situation, my father and his mother, but never had a clue about what the other was going through. It was something you never talked about.

I've heard it said that it's a small world. I find that to be a true statement. I found that you never know when or under what circumstance you will run into someone from your past. I believe it is not coincidence but ordained to happen.

With that said, it was meeting someone else that convinced me my higher power was God. I remember sitting in a circle at one particular meeting and looking at this young man. I kept getting this feeling that something was special about him. He was nice, friendly, but reserved.

It was weeks later when I saw him outside of a meeting at a very different location when I realized what was so special about him. He was a Catholic priest. He smiled at me and held his finger up to his lips, the shush signal. Again, Al-Anon is supposed to be anonymous.

I saw him for years after that, and we never discussed where we had first met.

I highly recommend this support group to anyone who is dealing with alcoholism in their family. It helped me learn how to cope, and as they say, "Keep coming back, it works."

I still repeat another phrase I learned from Al-Anon whenever I come up against a situation that is frustrating me and that I am trying to control: "Let go, and let God." It's a good time to pray and ask God for help.

When I got married and had children of my own, it was then that I realized that it's not just about me. God blessed me with two wonderful children to care for and to raise to be responsible people. Also when my parents got older, it was up to me to help them as much as I could.

We were created to help one another. That's why Al-Anon works. The people there share their story and spend time with you while you are struggling. They showed me how to cope when my life was so chaotic due to alcoholism.

Can you think of someone who might have helped you during a tough part of your life? Have you thought of helping someone else? You never know how just one kind word can work a miracle. When you help others, you are also helping yourself.

God tells us in the Bible why we are here and what we should be doing.

In the Old Testament, God gave Noah a set of rules for the people to follow, the Ten Commandments. But in the New Testament, when Jesus was questioned about the law, his response made it very clear: to love the Lord your God with all your heart, soul, and mind and to love your neighbor as yourself.

We were created by God in his image, and he wants us, his children, to spend eternity with him. So what are we called to do? The first thing we need to do is to honor God. We do this by seeking his kingdom.

God gave us written instructions on how we can do this. Everything we need to know about living life on this earth is in the Bible. Whatever questions you have, you can find the answer in the Bible.

When we attend church on Sundays, we show our heavenly Father that we are taking time out of our day to honor him. This starts our week off the right way. It shows God that we put him first and foremost.

Jesus tells us in Chapter 18 in the book of Matthew that when two or more are gathered in his name, he will be there. Gathering together with others to worship our Lord also gives us a sense of community that we are one people, not just one person struggling on their own. We are not meant to live this life alone. We are here to help one another live the best life we can.

By praying, we develop a closer relationship with him. Think of prayer as a conversation you are having with God. As a parent with adult children, I want to hear from them, how they are doing, and if there is something I can do to help them. It's the same with God. He wants to hear from you. He already knows what is going on in your life but wants to be a part of it.

When we tithe, we are giving God back what belongs to him. We show God that we understand that every good thing we have been given comes from him.

> But you are a chosen people, a royal priesthood, a holy nation, God's special possession, that you may declare the praises of him who called you out of darkness into his wonderful light. (1 Peter 2:9)

> But seek first his kingdom and his righteousness, and all these will be given to you as well. Therefore do not worry about tomorrow for tomorrow will worry about itself. Each day has enough trouble of its own. (Matthew 6:33–34)

When I start the day honoring God, praising him, and thanking him for all that he has given me, I find that my day goes well. Even if something does happen that I didn't expect, I am able to handle it without getting all stressed out. I realize that I don't have to do it all on my own. I have help from my heavenly Father.

Just remember that things are always changing, and to quote Scarlett O'Hara, "Tomorrow is another day."

Another way we honor God and why we were put on this earth is to be good to other people even when they are not good to us. We are called to be a light in a dark world.

"Do to others as you would have them do to you" (Luke 6:31).

"Do not withhold good from those to whom it is due, when it is in your power to act" (Proverbs 3:27).

"The King will reply, 'Truly I tell you, whatever you did for one of the least of these brothers and sisters of mine, you did for me'" (Matthew 25:40).

"Let us not become weary in doing good, for at the proper time we will reap a harvest if we do not give up" (Galatians 6:9).

This happens when we practice the fruits of the Holy Spirit: love, joy, peace, forbearance, kindness, goodness, faithfulness, gentleness, and self-control, which can be found in Galatians 5:22. Can you imagine what the world would be like if every person in the world followed this principle?

My son, Joe, told me about a situation that happened when he was in high school. There were a bunch of upperclassmen picking on a younger boy. It wasn't physical, but they taunted the boy so much that he was very upset.

As they were leaving, Joe, who was the same age as the bullies, went over to the boy and told him, "Don't listen to them. They are a bunch of idiots." That's all it took for the boy to smile back at him. There wasn't a fight, just a kind word.

Don't just walk by a situation if there is something you can do to make it better. Open the door for someone. Carry a bag of groceries for an elderly person. Offer someone the use of your phone if they need it. There is always something you can do to make someone else's life a little better. That's why we are here.

I know there are those who have wondered why they had ever been born. Maybe you were told that you were never wanted, or maybe that's how you feel.

I am here to say, "Please don't listen to whoever is saying this to you." You are wanted. You have a purpose and a reason for being here no matter what anyone tells you. Give yourself a break even when no one else does.

"For you created my inmost being; you knit me together in my mother's womb. I praise you because I am fearfully and wonderfully made; your works are wonderful, I know that full well" (Psalm 139:13–14).

We are all human beings, but we are also unique individuals with our own DNA and fingerprints. This means no two people are alike, even identical twins. We may look like someone else, but we are not the same person.

There is a quote I really like, and it is credited to the Irish playwright Oscar Wilde although he may not have actually said it. It goes, "Be yourself; everyone else is already taken."

You can see God's intent in the verses from 1 Corinthians shown below.

"Just as a body, though one, has many parts, but all its many parts form one body, so it is with Christ" (1 Corinthians 12:12).

"Now you are the body of Christ, and each one of you is a part of it" (1 Corinthians 12:27).

Each of us has special gifts and is called for a special purpose, everyone. We were all created by God—the good, the bad, and the ugly. We all have a reason for being alive. God doesn't make mistakes. It's what we do with our gifts that makes all the difference.

"'For I know the plans I have for you,' declares the Lord, 'Plans to prosper you and not to harm you, plans to give you hope and a future'" (Jeremiah 29:11).

"There are different kinds of gifts, but the same Spirit distributes them" (1 Corinthians 12:4).

Mary had a profound purpose, to be the mother of Jesus Christ, our Savior.

John the Baptist was born to prepare the way for Jesus.

I have discovered that my gifts include being a good support system for others. When I look at my life, I can see it very clearly now. It's why I enjoy playing bass guitar in a big band. The bass is part of the rhythm section and supports the other instruments. We get to entertain seniors living in assisted-living facilities with live music.

I remember one time as we were playing a song, there was an elderly woman sitting in a recliner. I saw her start singing quietly to herself. When the song was over, she went back to her previous comatose state. I like to think that at least for a couple of minutes, it brought her some joy and maybe brought back some special memories.

I enjoy crocheting and recently joined a crochet group at our church. We make hats and scarves to give as gifts to those who are homeless and in need. In New Jersey, the months of November through March can get very cold, so these come in handy. I'm doing something I enjoy and am able to bless others with what I make.

And nothing brings me greater joy than helping others achieve their goals. When both of my children graduated from college, I couldn't have been happier knowing I was there to help them when they needed me. They have made me so proud.

It took me years to discover my purpose. And I am still finding new ways to use the gifts that God has given me. When you find yours and you will, you'll know it. It's like everything now makes sense. Remember, you are unique, one of a kind, and created by a loving God.

One of the ways you will know you are headed in the right direction is that God will put people in your path that will help you along the way. He has a purpose for you, and he will help you see it through. All you need to do is start doing what you feel he is calling you to do.

As I have been writing this book, I have received guidance and encouragement from other people. The best and most amazing part is that God reunited me with someone from my past, an old friend. We ran into each other in the grocery store by chance and hadn't seen each other in over thirty years.

Turns out she had written not one but two books that have been published, *Secondhand Scotch*, available through Amazon, and *The Funny Side of the Street*, through Xlibris. She has been through both sides: self-publishing and with a publisher. Since I have not done this before, she was very forthcoming with her knowledge of the process.

God is always directing our steps in order for us to have the best life possible and to help others. I found this Bible passage that is especially relevant to me at this time in my life. Now that I am retired, it is a good reminder of what God expects of me.

"Likewise, teach the older women to be reverent in the way they live, not to be slanderers or addicted to much wine, but to teach what is good" (Titus 2:3).

Warning: not everyone will celebrate you and what you accomplish, however. They may become jealous of what you have or your situation. They may want or expect you to do something that was not meant for you to do.

There is a very popular TV evangelist who has received criticism because of where he lives and how much money his ministry has acquired. They wonder why he doesn't use the money to eliminate hunger and help the poor of this world. But his church does have a ministry that addresses this issue, and even still, they feel that he's not doing enough.

It is stated very clearly in the Bible that this is not a problem that can be eliminated. The Gospels of Matthew, Mark, and John all speak of the poor and how they will always be among us and that it is up to all of us to do what we can to help them, not just the rich people.

"A generous person will prosper; whoever refreshes others will be refreshed" (Proverbs 11:25).

"Whoever oppresses the poor shows contempt for their Maker, but whoever is kind to the needy honors God" (Proverbs 14:31).

This man has a different calling and is following it. Through his ministry, so many of God's people have heard his Word and have been saved. That is another thing we are all called to do. We plant the seed, and God will do the rest.

"Therefore, go and make disciples of all nations, baptizing them in the name of the Father and of the Son and of the Holy Spirit" (Matthew 28:19).

"I tell you, whoever publicly acknowledges me before others, the Son of Man will also acknowledge before the angels of God" (Luke 12:8).

"Let your light shine before others, that they may see your good deeds and glorify your Father in heaven" (Matthew 5:16).

We also have to remember that this man will be judged at a higher standard than most of us.

"From everyone who has been given much, much will be demanded; and from the one who has been entrusted with much, much more will be asked" (Luke 12:48).

So you are here because God wanted you here. You are here to serve God and to serve others.

He has a plan for your life, and if you don't know that yet, pray and ask for God's guidance. He will direct your steps.

"Trust in the Lord with all your heart and lean not on your own understanding; in all your ways submit to him, and he will make your paths straight" (Proverbs 3:5–6).

Now, here are some questions for you to think about: What do you enjoy doing? What brings you joy and makes you feel good? How can you turn that into a way to honor God and help others?

"Each of you should use whatever gift you have received to serve others, as faithful stewards of God's grace in its various forms" (1 Peter 4:10).

# CHAPTER 6

～～～

# *How Do I Pray?*

*Is anyone among you in trouble? Let them pray. Is anyone happy?
Let them sing songs of praise. Is anyone among you sick? Let them
call the elders of the church to pray over them and anoint them
with oil in the name of the Lord. And the prayer offered in faith
will make the sick person well; the Lord will raise them up. If
they have sinned they will be forgiven. Therefore confess your sins
to each other and pray for each other so that you may be healed.
The prayer of a righteous person is powerful and effective.*

—James 5:13–16

Some people are not familiar with praying. They have never done it or have never been shown how to. Let me start by saying, "Anyone can and should pray." It doesn't matter who you are, what you've done, and where you are in life. God will listen.

Prayer is a conversation you have with God. It is a way to build a relationship with him and to get closer to him. It can be with a group, in a church setting, or a private time between you and God. You can stand, walk around, and even sit, but the best way is on your knees. That gives God the honor and respect that he deserves.

Prayer can be a way to give God praise, to thank him, to repent and ask forgiveness, and to ask him for help as shown above in the

Bible passage found in the book of James. We were not meant to go through this world on our own. God wants his children to come to him.

Here is an example of a very simple prayer: Heavenly Father, thank you for this day. All glory and honor belong to you. Please watch over me and my family today, and help me do the right things that honor you. In Jesus's name, amen.

The Holy Spirit intercedes for us even when we don't know what to pray for.

> In the same way, the Spirit helps us in our weakness. We do not know what we ought to pray for, but the Spirit himself intercedes for us through wordless groans. And he who searches our hearts knows the mind of the Spirit, because the Spirit intercedes for God's people in accordance with the will of God. (Romans 8:26–27)

All you need to do is start the conversation. God wants to hear from you. As a parent, I know how I feel when one of my children or grandchildren calls me. The reason doesn't matter. It's just good to hear their voice and know they are thinking of me.

When you wake up every morning, thank God for a wonderful new day and that you're alive to enjoy it. It doesn't matter how long you pray. Just that you do.

"But God has surely listened and has heard my prayer" (Psalm 66:19).

If something good happens, you find money on the sidewalk or you get a promotion, whatever it is, say a quick prayer of thanks.

"Thank you, Lord, for this gift!" Every good thing comes from God.

Just the other day, my son asked me if I smelled gas. It turned out that the gas burner on the stove was still on but with no flame. So it was quickly turned off. If he didn't notice or didn't say anything, who knows what could have happened in the house and to us. I thanked God for making us aware of the situation and for the quick resolution.

Think about how you felt after giving someone a gift. Did they say "Thank you"? How did it make you feel? For me, when I know someone is grateful for something I gave them or did for them, it makes me feel good, and I want to do more.

There is a saying that goes, "It is better to give than to receive." Of course, when you were a child, this did not make sense. Children are born selfish and for good reason. It's part of the instinct to survive. But as they grow and learn how to take care of themselves, it becomes easier for them to let go of those selfish feelings.

Unfortunately, some adults are still struggling to survive. Pray for them and their situation, and see if there is something you can do to help them. You might be the answer to their prayer.

If you are anxious, remember to place God first and foremost and ask for his help and guidance.

> Do not be anxious about anything, but
> in every situation, by prayer and petition, with
> thanksgiving, present your requests to God. And
> the peace of God, which transcends all under-
> standing will guard your hearts and your minds
> in Christ Jesus. (Philippians 4:6–7)

If something bad happens, ask God for his help. Ask for his grace and mercy. Ask for his strength to help you get through this time. He wants to help but will step back if you try to handle it on your own.

"He will respond to the prayer of the destitute; he will not despise their plea" (Psalm 102:17)

Prayer is not only for you. Remember the people that touch your life, and ask God to watch over them. When others are suffering, that's a perfect time to offer a prayer for them.

Most churches provide an opportunity for people to receive prayer for whatever reason, depending on their circumstances. In the Catholic church, you can light candles, and in most nondenominational churches, they will have a prayer leader who will pray with you during a church service.

Some churches have published prayer lists with people's names that you can pray for. I have seen them in weekly church bulletins, God's people praying for others.

Jesus prayed for his disciples.

"I pray for them. I am not praying for the world, but for those you have given me, for they are yours" (John 17:9).

"My prayer is not that you take them out of the world, but that you protect them from the evil one" (John 17:15).

When you pray, make sure you do it in Jesus's name. That is how you reach the Father.

"Very truly I tell you, my Father will give you whatever you ask in my name" (John 16:23).

This was what Jesus instructed at the Sermon on the Mount:

> This, then, is how you should pray:
> Our Father in heaven,
> Hallowed be your name,
> Your kingdom come,
> Your will be done,
> On earth as it is in heaven.
> Give us today our daily bread.
> And forgive us our debts,
> As we also have forgiven our debtors,
> And lead us not into temptation,
> But deliver us from the evil one. (Matthew 6:9–13)

There is a wonderful book on prayers written by Pastor D. Qwynn Gross. It is called *Frame Your World* and was published by Steadfast Hope Publishing. There are prayers to help anyone through situations in their life such as anger, a broken heart, bullying, divorce, being jobless, depression, sexual identity, and weariness.

Pray with a thankful heart. Tell God that you are grateful for all he has given you. Pray with the knowledge that God hears you. Pray for your needs and for others. Pray for strength. Pray for wisdom to discern right from wrong. Pray for patience. Pray for peace. Pray for God's mercy.

Just pray!

C H A P T E R   7

# Does God Answer Prayers?

*Ask and it will be given to you; seek and you will find; knock and the door will be opened to you. For everyone who asks receives; the one who seeks finds; and to the one who knocks, the door will be opened.*

—Matthew 7:7–8

Why doesn't God answer my prayers? When will he answer my prayers?

God answers prayers: sometimes, the answer is yes, and the result is almost instantaneous.

My very dear friend ended a relationship with a guy she was seeing. She was so distraught. We had talked on the phone, and when we hung up, I started praying for her. I wanted God to remove her sadness and bring her peace of mind, so that is what I prayed for.

A couple of days later, we were talking, and I asked her how she was doing. She said that she was doing really good, and the funniest thing happened. After we talked the last time, all of a sudden, she felt all the unhappiness just lift from her shoulders. All the sadness disappeared.

Years ago, I remember my son and his father got two tickets to a New York Jets football game. The last time they went somewhere, just the two of them, his father had too much to drink, and he was driving. I was worried that this might happen again, so I prayed and asked God for help.

That weekend, his uncle asked if we'd be interested in four Jets tickets for the exact same game. Thank you, God! We enjoyed the game, and I drove home. God changed the scenario and made it possible for all of us to attend together and drive safely home.

"If you believe, you will receive whatever you ask for in prayer" (Matthew 21:22).

Sometimes, the answer is no. Check your heart. What are you asking for, and what is the reason behind it?

"You do not have because you do not ask God. When you ask, you do not receive, because you ask with wrong motives…" (James 4:2–3).

Another thing to consider is, are you asking for something you need or something you want? As seen in the scripture below, it talks about God meeting your needs.

So what is the difference? As humans, we have basic needs in order to survive—air to breathe, water to drink, food to eat, clothing, and shelter. We also have other needs in order to feel good about ourselves such as companionship, a sense of belonging, and feeling of self-worth.

A want is more of a desire or wish for something. Are you asking for a need or a want?

Let's consider this example. I need a car so that I have transportation to and from work. I need to work in order to feed my family and pay my rent. With the car, I can pick my children up after school and go grocery shopping.

Maybe God sends someone your way that has an old clunker that's in good running condition that you can have, but you are ashamed of how it looks. You want a nice car. There is nothing wrong with wanting something better, but don't ignore what has come your way. Be thankful, and God will give you more. If we are not grateful for what he has already given, why should he give us more?

I remember hearing this story about two men that were talking. The first complained about everything that was happening to him.

He told his friend that he didn't think it could get any worse. So God showed him how much worse it could be.

The second man had nothing but good things to say. He told his friend how it couldn't get any better than this. So God showed him how much better it could be.

This made me really think about perspective. Yes, you may be facing some trials right now, but don't focus on that. Change your view, and look at the good things God has given you, and thank him for it.

"And my God will meet all your needs according to the riches of his glory in Christ Jesus" (Philippians 4:19).

And sometimes, the answer is no, and we may not know the reason why.

This is what happened to me when I tried seven different times to change positions in the company I worked for. I put in application after application for entry-level positions and couldn't understand why I didn't get any of them when I was fully qualified. I prayed and prayed, but the answer was no each and every time. What I didn't know is that God had a better plan for me.

After several years, it became clear why the answer was no. The "something better" was not available yet. Our heavenly Father always wants what is best for us, just like parents want what is best for their child.

That leads me to answer number three. It's going to happen, but we have to have patience and trust. This is where relying on your faith comes in. God may need time to work everything out.

Abraham and Sarah waited twenty-five years before Isaac was born. They tried their own way to bring about what God had promised them, but that was not what they were supposed to do.

It took the Israelites forty years to reach the promised land due to their disobedience. They created a calf of gold and worshipped it instead of God. They should have spent the time praying instead.

In the book of Daniel, an angel of God was delayed twenty-one days before he was able to meet with Daniel in answer to his prayers. The angel was busy in a battle with the prince of the Persian kingdom. During that time, Daniel fasted and prayed. His prayers were answered.

"Hope deferred makes the heart sick, but a longing fulfilled is a tree of life" (Proverbs 13:12).

"Be still before the Lord and wait patiently for him;…" (Psalm 37:7).

Several years later, the right position became available, and it was mine. The company I was currently working for decided to spin off its hospital-products division. That move opened up the perfect spot for me.

During this time of waiting and after I got the new position, I continued to increase my knowledge and obtained my four-year college degree and then my customs broker's license.

Because I continued to grow, I was promoted six times. The first four promotions happened within three years, which is unprecedented for almost anyone working for any company. My manager, who was responsible for making it happen, was still amazed at how quickly I was promoted. Then I was given a supervisory role.

Our company was acquired a couple of years later, and I was promoted again to a manager position. This took place within a few months after the acquisition. Several years later, I was able to retire and feel confident about my future.

I say this not to brag on me but to show how God blessed me with his goodness. When people are successful, there is always a reason. Yes, I did a lot to get to where I am today, but I couldn't have done it without God. He placed people, opportunities, and other things within my path that helped me get to where I ended up.

While you are waiting for your answer, don't be idle and expect God to do it all. The delay might be because we are not prepared for what is to come.

At the time of writing this book, our world has been going through the COVID-19 pandemic. People have been praying to God for help, and I believe he answered us by providing not one but two vaccines that were developed using new technologies. These vaccines became available within one year.

Creating a vaccine takes years to develop, so people have been suspicious as to the safety and efficacy of the vaccines. However, these technologies were in development at least a decade before the pandemic hit. I know because I worked for one of the companies that was able to provide it without government money.

What they needed to do was to make some modifications and perform clinical trials. Once those steps were completed, the vaccines were able to receive emergency-use approval from the FDA and be distributed.

God already knew what was going to happen, and when we all prayed, he responded.

"For your Father knows what you need before you ask him" (Matthew 6:8).

We put our faith and trust in so many things, such as that the chair we are about to sit on will hold our body. But I have seen several people fall through chairs that were worn out from age or that have broken legs so it could not support the weight.

Some people trust the government for that social security check every month. Can we feel comfortable that the money will always be there for us?

I thank God for GPS to help me navigate to the places I want to go. I remember writing down directions and usually still getting lost and having to call my husband to help me. But I don't put my trust in it because there are times that the directions are contrary. I may know a shortcut, or maybe I don't want to pay tolls and will go five minutes out of my way.

Others put their trust in people, but people can let you down. People are not perfect and make mistakes.

When you prayed, did you believe that you will receive it? Sometimes, we pray as the last resort thinking that it probably won't happen. The problem is, if that is how you are thinking, then you are right. It probably won't happen.

"Therefore I tell you, whatever you ask for in prayer, believe that you have received it, and it will be yours" (Mark 11:24).

What have you asked for and received? Did you thank God for it? What have you asked for and did not receive? I suggest you look at the request very carefully. Was this a need or a want? Did you ask with the right motive? Did you believe God would provide it? Is it something that may take time, and are you doing all you can while waiting for God to respond?

The decision of when to retire from my job took a lot of praying and waiting for God to let me know when the right time was. I did not have a pension, so there was no time frame that I had to follow.

I live in New Jersey and close to a major university. Their symbol is a big red "R." That became my reminder that retirement was on the way. So every time I saw a car drive by with the big red "R," I thanked God that my retirement was coming.

During that waiting period, I put together a financial plan. I wrote down all our future assets, which included everything we had saved, and subtracted out our debt and future bills. I determined that when I was at the age social security considered full retirement age, sixty-six and two months, and started collecting then, we would have enough to live on. What we had in our 401(k) would cover travel twice a year to visit Dan's family in the Midwest and any outstanding expenses we might incur.

God provided the means, and his timing was perfect. I retired when I turned sixty-six and two months! We celebrated by spending two weeks at a beach house in South Carolina with our families.

Put your faith and trust in God. He never makes mistakes. Keep praying and believing! You will get your answer. It may not be the one you are looking for, but God will always give you his best.

# CHAPTER 8

## Why Did God Let This Happen?

*I have seen something else under the sun:*
*The race is not to the swift*
*Or the battle to the strong,*
*Nor does food come to the wise*
*Or wealth to the brilliant*
*Or favor to the learned;*
*But time and chance happen to them all.*

—Ecclesiastes 9:11

"I have told you these things, so that in me you may have peace, in this world you will have trouble. But take heart! I have overcome the world" (John 16:33).

People are always asking, "If God is so good, why do bad things happen?"

I got married for the first time when I was twenty-two years old. I believed in God and wanted to be married and have a family. I was blessed with two children, and as hard as I tried, I could not make my marriage work. It was not an easy decision to file for divorce, but I knew I had to.

I ended up moving from my home to a different state in order to financially support my children and give them the opportunity to attend college, something I knew would enhance their future. No one in our family had a college degree.

"'For I know the plans I have for you,' declares the Lord, 'plans to prosper you and not to harm you, plans to give you hope and a future'" (Jeremiah 29:11).

"And we know that in all things God works for the good of those who love him, who have been called according to his purpose" (Romans 8:28).

Things happen, good and bad. When good things happen, we think it's good luck. We are in the right place at the right time. But all good things come from God. He is the one who arranges for us to be in the right place. He is the one who determines the right time. Did we thank Him for our good fortune?

"Every good and perfect gift is from above, coming down from the Father of the heavenly lights, who does not change like shifting shadows" (James 1:17).

However, when bad things happen to them, people look for someone to blame, and they usually look up. God, why did you do this, or God, why didn't you do anything to stop it?

God never said we would have an idyllic life with no trouble, but when trouble came, he would be there to help us through it. Having faith in God will help us get through the storms we are facing. Faith is believing and trusting in God.

"'Have faith in God,' Jesus answered" (Mark 11:22).

"The Lord is a refuge for the oppressed, a stronghold in times of trouble. Those who know your name trust in you, for you, Lord, have never forsaken those who seek you" (Psalm 9:9–10).

"For I am the Lord your God who takes hold of your right hand and says to you, Do not fear; I will help you" (Isaiah 41:13).

He does however allow us to be tested. Why? Sometimes for us to learn some type of lesson but most times we don't know. God has his reasons, and one day, they will be revealed to us. A good example of this is the story of Job.

"This man was blameless and upright; he feared God and shunned evil" (Job 1:1).

Satan appeared one day with God's angels after roaming the earth. This is what he does, looking to stir up trouble. When God told him about Job, Satan replied, "It's only because you have a hedge of protection around him."

Satan recognizes who belongs to God and will try everything to break that connection.

The Lord told Satan that everything Job had would be in Satan's power, but he was not to touch Job.

That's what we have to remember. The trouble is not coming from God. God cannot be tempted by evil and doesn't tempt anyone. We are tempted by our own evil desire. God can help us overcome it.

"He will cover you with his feathers, and under his wings you will find refuge; his faithfulness will be your shield and rampart" (Psalm 90:4).

Even though Satan caused Job to lose everything, Job still continued to fear God and worship him even though he did not understand why the trouble was upon him. He had faith that God would bring him through all the trouble.

Even Job's wife told him to curse God and die.

His reply is one we should take to heart and remember always.

"He replied, 'You are talking like a foolish woman. Shall we accept good from God, and not trouble?' In all this, Job did not sin in what he said" (Job 2:10).

The Lord restored all Job's fortune and gave him twice as much as he had before. The second half of Job's life was better than the first.

What I have learned from the book of Job is to thank God for the good and to trust him when trouble comes, and it will.

"I can do all this through him who gives me strength" (Philippians 4:13).

"The righteous person may have many troubles, but the Lord delivers him from them all" (Psalm 34:19).

Several years ago, our pastor went through his own trial. He was arrested for what was considered financial fraud having to do with a credit union he established to help those in need. I don't have all the details, but I know it is in the public records.

The trial was held in New York City, not locally because it was easier to get a conviction even though the supposed crime was in New Jersey. The elders of the church were told they would be open to the same criminal prosecution if they testified on his behalf even though they had met voluntarily with the government a year before and answered all their questions. I am told this is a tactic used to remove a defense from someone because it takes away their witnesses.

He ended up being sentenced to five years in prison. People that commit more heinous crimes get off with a lot less. I don't understand why the federal court and this particular judge were so harsh. However, what I do know is that God must have had a purpose for this.

While our pastor was in prison, he continued to minister to God's people but now in a different location and to a new congregation. His wife and the elders continued the ministry, and the church continued to thrive although several members left. So people were being fed now from two places, instead of just one. What the enemy meant for evil was turned to good because our pastor remained faithful to God.

The church continued to pray for him, his wife, and his family. His wife prayed continually. My personal prayer was that he returns to us as soon as possible.

Then, like Paul and Silas in the book of Acts and due to the COVID-19 pandemic, he was released early, and our church has been on the rebound, thriving and growing again.

This was a test, and we all passed. This was an attack, and we all came through. Like Job, our pastor remained faithful to God. He continued the ministry and reached souls that might not have heard the word otherwise. Our church leaders along with the congregation remained faithful and kept praying.

God knows your pain. He sent his only Son to earth and watched Jesus suffer and die on the cross. He did this because of his love for us, and can we honestly say we deserve it? Would we sacrifice ourselves or, even worse, our own child for this world?

Remember, people were created having free will, a choice. There are those who choose to follow the evil one or are easily influenced by him. This is why bad things happen. It is a daily struggle which voice to listen to. For some, it's harder than others.

"For our struggle is not against flesh and blood, but against the rulers, against the authorities, against the powers of this dark world and against the spiritual forces of evil in the heavenly realms" (Ephesians 6:12).

When Jesus is led by the Holy Spirit into the wilderness, He is tempted by the devil. In exchange for worshipping him instead of God, Satan offers Jesus the world.

> The devil led him up to a high place and showed him in an instant all the kingdoms of the world. And he said to him, "I will give you all their authority and splendor; it has been given to me, and I can give it to anyone I want to. If you worship me, it will all be yours." (Luke 4:5)

I recently watched a movie where a father is on a camping trip with his kids and the youngest girl ends up getting kidnapped and killed by a psychopath. He asks God why he would allow this to happen and how God can leave her all alone. But God told the man that his daughter was never alone and that he was with her always.

When Jesus was crucified, God was there with his Son.

"Be strong and courageous. Do not be afraid or terrified because of them, for the Lord your God goes with you; he will never leave you nor forsake you" (Deuteronomy 31:6).

God helps the man grieve for his daughter and eventually to forgive. This is not an easy thing to do. But we need to forgive in order for us to heal. The ability to forgive someone that has done us wrong is for us so that we can move forward. It is not good for us to hold onto things that have hurt us.

"Blessed are those who mourn, for they will be comforted" (Matthew 5:4).

"The Lord is close to the brokenhearted and saves those who are crushed in spirit" (Psalm 34:18).

How do you forgive someone who had done evil against you? Ask God to help you. God knows what it's like to suffer, seeing Jesus make the ultimate sacrifice as the only way for God's people to be with him in heaven.

God suffers when his children continue to do evil and end up in hell.

"And when you stand praying, if you hold anything against anyone, forgive them, so that your Father in heaven may forgive you your sins" (Mark 11:25).

Keep your eyes on God, and he will bring you through whatever it is you are going through. Leave what you're feeling: your sorrow, pain, hatred, anger with him. He will handle it.

Feelings are always changing and can lead us in the wrong direction. We need to have faith in God in everything. God is our vindicator. He tells us not to repay evil for evil but to do what is right.

"The Lord will vindicate his people and relent concerning his servants when he sees their strength is gone and no one is left, slave or free" (Deuteronomy 32:36).

"For we know him who said, 'It is mine to avenge; I will repay,' and again, 'The Lord will judge his people'" (Hebrews 10:30).

In the book of James, we are told that we should consider it pure joy whenever we face trials because the testing of our faith produces perseverance.

"Blessed is the one who perseveres under trial because, having stood the test, that person will receive the crown of life that the Lord has promised to those who love him" (James 1:12).

This life is not easy. There is evil everywhere. But we have a loving God that wants to help us through it if we let him.

Take this time to examine your heart. Is there someone you need to forgive? Do it now so you can be cleansed and can move forward. Forgiveness is for you. God will avenge whatever the wrong that was done. Trust Him.

My girlfriend, Cathy, gave me permission to share this poem that she had written, and I hope it touches you as much as it did me:

## DEAR GOD

Dear God,
Can you hear me?
I don't mean to be so rude,
But how come there are children here
With hardly any food?
How come wars are raging?
And what about the crime?
And what about the kid next door
Who's rotten all the time?
What about the children
Who haven't got a mother?
And what about the brother
Who hasn't got a dime?
I will rest me head now.
My soul is Yours to keep,
But answer all my questions,
So that I can get some sleep.
Love,
Ruth

Dear Ruth,
You are quite precocious.
And your questions weren't rude.
Quite frankly, they were actually,
Really very good.
I know lots of things need fixing
In the world that you are living,
But that's to be accomplished
Through people—Sharing, Loving, Giving.
'Cause if I started fixing
What might break before it's broken,
You'd have Heaven there on earth,
And that includes Hoboken.
So, I think I'll keep My Heaven
Way up here where angels roam
But anytime that you invite Me,

I'll come into your home.
More importantly, remember
That I've given you Free Will;
No one is forced to follow Me,
And better, better still:
My favorite, little children
Are those who seek the truth,
With courage to ask questions,
Like you, My Baby, Ruth.
Love,
God

# CHAPTER 9

# Why Is the Church Always Asking for Money?

A tithe of everything from the land, whether grain from the soil or fruit from the trees, belongs to the Lord; it is holy to the Lord.

—Leviticus 27:30

Will a mere mortal rob God? Yet you rob me. But you ask, "How are we robbing you?"

"In tithes and offerings. You are under a curse-your whole nation-because you are robbing me. Bring the whole tithe into the storehouse, that there may be food in my house. Test me in this," says the Lord Almighty, "and see if I will not throw open the floodgates of heaven and pour out so much blessing that there will not be room enough to store it. I will prevent pests from devouring your crops, and the vines in your fields will not drop their fruit before it is ripe," says the Lord Almighty. "Then all the nations will call you blessed, for yours will be a delightful land," says the Lord Almighty. (Malachi 3:8–12)

What is a tithe? I like how one of my pastors explains it: it's one-tenth of your increase. All we have comes from God, and all he wants in return is the first 10 percent. That means 90 percent is ours.

Although it may seem like the church is always asking for money, that is not the case. I remember feeling the same way. Why do they keep asking for money? Why are there always not one but two envelopes? It wasn't until I truly understood that it's what God expects us to do that I stopped feeling this way.

When a poor widow put two small copper coins in the offering, this is what Jesus said:

> Calling his disciples to him, Jesus said, "Truly I tell you, this poor widow has put more into the treasury than all the others. They all gave out of their wealth; but she, out of her poverty, put in everything-all she had to live on." (Mark 12:43–44)

I like this passage because it is a reminder of what is important, not how much money we have or what we give but trusting God and following him. That is what the widow did.

The giving should be with a cheerful heart because we love God and want to do the right thing.

> Each of you should give what you have decided in your heart to give, not reluctantly or under compulsion, for God loves a cheerful giver. And God is able to bless you abundantly, so that in all things at all times, having all you need, you will abound in every good work. (2 Corinthians 9:7–8)

When I was working, I would give 10 percent of my take-home pay as my tithe. Now it is 10 percent of my social security. If I play a gig and am paid in cash, I give 10 percent of that. If I am given a gift of money, I will give God 10 percent of that. Whatever God has blessed me with, I return to him through my church, and I have received more than I have ever given. God is true to his Word.

I was a single parent at one time and didn't make much money. However, I was able to pay for not only both my children to go to college but also myself. I kept faithful to God, and he provided a way when I didn't think it would be possible.

For example, it was during that time that some tax deductions changed, and I was able to get back more in my tax return than I had originally paid.

Ever since I have been tithing, my needs have always been met. I don't have to worry about money and am able to bless others. There is a joy that comes from tithing, receiving from it, and then being able to bless other people because of it.

I am a cheerful giver, but it did take time to get there. I can always think of other ways that money can be used. But then I remember that God provided the means, a good-paying job, so I give back what belongs to God.

"Give, and it will be given to you. A good measure, pressed down, shaken together and running over, will be poured into your lap. For with the measure you use, it will be measured to you" (Luke 6:38).

Isn't an offering the same? What's the difference? No, an offering is not the tithe. An offering is something you give freely, over and above the tithe. An example would be if your church hosted a visiting missionary, and you gave a special offering to help their cause. Or maybe your church is sponsoring a food drive or Angel Tree.

When you bring food or a gift, that would be an offering. It is out of the portion God has given to you for your needs, a portion of the 90 percent.

An offering is a way to bless others from the abundance we have been given. When someone asks of us, we should give what we can. It should never be a hardship.

Giving is part of the principle of sowing and reaping. There are many ways to sow a seed besides giving money. I found that when I volunteer my time, I find myself with more time to do what I want to do. This includes being able to retire comfortably.

I've spent time volunteering in soup kitchens and have never gone hungry.

I enjoy giving gifts, especially on the spur of the moment and have received back gifts that are so special they touch my heart.

Over the years, I have donated clothing for several reasons: it doesn't fit me anymore, I'm tired of it, I bought it but never wear it, etc. It's no surprise to me that I have reaped a closet full of clothes, and when I do go shopping, it never fails that I find something that fits great, looks good on me, and, best of all, is on sale.

I remember the days when we lived paycheck to paycheck, not sure we'd have enough to get by. There was a time we belonged to a food-distribution program that was run by the government. They would hand out different items: vegetables, blocks of cheese, and cornmeal, for example. I learned to make bread with cornmeal. We ate a lot of grilled-cheese sandwiches.

But I remained faithful to God with my tithe, and he brought me out of that difficult financial situation into a life of more than enough.

My family is living proof that 2 Corinthians speaks the truth.

Here is a suggestion. Try tithing for a year, and see if your life has taken a turn for the better. It's God's promise to all of us.

# CHAPTER 10

## Can Anyone Be Saved?

*Salvation is found in no one else, for there is no other name
under heaven given to mankind by which we must be saved.*

—Acts 4:12

What does salvation mean, being saved from what? We are being saved from a life of sin and of eternal death and damnation. Jesus died for us so that we could be reunited with the Father and be able to join him in heaven to live for all eternity.

When you go through the process of salvation, it means your old life, your sinful life, is gone, and you start fresh.

Can anyone be saved? The answer is yes if you believe and are willing to follow the steps that are required.

You have to recognize the wrongs you have done, feel sorrow for it, commit that you will not do it again, take action to prevent it from happening again, and fix the problem if you can. If we injured another person, we should make restitution. This is called repentance.

This also includes forgiving others that have sinned against us.

People are not perfect, and we all make mistakes even when we try not to. Maybe someone hurt us, and it is hard to get over it, but we have probably done the same thing to someone else. Did we ask for forgiveness? Did we even realize we did it?

I remember talking to a coworker and saying something very stupid, not thinking about what was coming out of my mouth. I didn't realize it at the time, but when what I said finally dawned on me, I went back and apologized for it. I could have just let it go, but it wouldn't have been right. When you feel remorse, do the right thing. This is repentance.

"For if you forgive other people when they sin against you, your heavenly Father will also forgive you. But if you do not forgive others their sins, your Father will not forgive your sins" (Matthew 6:14–15).

Don't look to get even for wrong or seek revenge. God has assured us that it will be taken care of. You have to trust and have faith.

Have there been times in your life that someone did you wrong? Did anything come of it?

When I was at a specific job, I was reporting to a supervisor who had a knack for making you feel less than because of the lower position you had with the company. My coworker at the time was very resentful, and I have to admit so was I even though I tried to let it go.

We still did the best job we could do but did a lot of complaining. We were both Christians, and we knew better. I regret my actions, but God still looked on me with favor.

Eventually, through his grace and mercy, I was promoted several times and ended up with a higher position than that supervisor. Once that happened, she treated me differently.

"Be sure of this: The wicked will not go unpunished, but those who are righteous will go free" (Proverbs 11:21).

Once you recognize the sin(s) and repent, ask God to forgive you.

Next, you must accept into your heart that Jesus is your Lord and Savior and make that verbal declaration.

We make that declaration every Sunday in the church I belong to, and we say it together as a united body. It's a good reminder for all of us.

Finally, you need to be baptized in the name of the Father, Son, and Holy Spirit. Baptism is the full emersion of your body in water.

It is a sign that sin is washed away. Jesus was baptized by John the Baptist even though he had no sin.

"Peter replied, "Repent and be baptized, every one of you, in the name of Jesus Christ for the forgiveness of your sins. And you will receive the gift of the Holy Spirit" (Acts 2:38).

When I was born, my mother and father had me christened. This is not the same thing as being baptized because it only requires a sprinkling of water on the head.

My parents had me baptized at the age of seven, in the Russian Orthodox Church, along with my sister and my mother. No one asked if I wanted to do this, and I didn't really understand what it meant.

It wasn't until I was seventeen and I fully accepted Jesus Christ as my savior, understanding what this meant, that I decided to be baptized and become a Christian. I went to a local lake with a few other people from my church so that I could be water baptized, fully immersed.

I don't remember who baptized me, but I do remember feeling refreshed and renewed.

At baptism, you will receive the gift of the Holy Spirit, and your life will never be the same. You are now a true child of God.

Does that mean if you sin after that, you lose your salvation? It's possible, however, God knows that we are all sinners and have a sinful nature. It's his grace and mercy that we need to pray for because we will be judged for it. Also, we need to repent each and every time.

Humans have a sinful nature, but we have to fight it. God is reaching for us, but so is the enemy.

> If we deliberately keep on sinning after we
> have received the knowledge of the truth, no sac-
> rifice for sins is left, but only a fearful expectation
> of judgement and of raging fire that will consume
> the enemies of God. (Hebrews 10:26–27)

Sometimes, a Christian can be "stuck" and keep committing the same sin. It does not mean all is lost as long as you are sincerely trying your best to overcome it. Pray and ask God for his strength and mercy. Keep the lines of communication open. He will give you what you ask for.

What we have to remember is that this life we are living on earth is temporary, and God wants us to have a future with him. That's why he sent his only Son to be crucified so that we may be reconciled to our Father.

"I tell you that in the same way there will be more rejoicing in heaven over one sinner who repents than over ninety-nine righteous persons who do not need to repent" (Luke 15:7).

There is a story in the book of Luke known as the Prodigal Son. It tells of a father that had two sons. The older one was faithful and did what his father asked, but the younger one asks for his inheritance and then leaves. He ends up squandering all of it and becomes destitute. He returns home and begs his father to accept him back as a servant.

The father welcomes him back with open arms and has a celebration. His brother is envious and says that he never did that for him. But the father explains that while he was always with him and everything he has is his, his brother was lost and is now found. It was like he was dead but now is alive again.

This is the story of redemption that no matter what we have done, God will accept us back with celebration.

This is God's amazing grace.

# CHAPTER 11

## I'm Saved, Now What?

*Remember the Sabbath day by keeping it holy.*

—Exodus 20:8

Once you are saved, your journey does not end. It begins. This is the time to draw closer to God and become a true follower of Christ. We do this by praying, reading the Bible, and coming together with others to praise and worship our Lord as one body. We attend church on Sunday to show God we are obedient and that we honor Him.

So you should find a church if you have not done it already. You need to be connected to other believers. It usually takes a while to find a place that feels right. It is important that the church and its pastor(s) are able to fill you up with what you need.

When you do a google search, you will find lots of choices. This is a good thing although it does not make it any easier to find the right place. There are well over three hundred thousand churches in the United States, and each town I'm sure has several choices depending on denomination. I suggest finding a Christian church that bases their teachings on the Bible.

When I was young, our family belonged to the Russian Orthodox Church, first in Kentucky when my dad was still in the army and stationed in Fort Knox then when we moved back to New Jersey to a church close to our home.

My father's family was Russian Orthodox, so that is where he felt comfortable. I never understood it, so I didn't care for attending the services although we went for my father's sake.

When I started dating this guy in high school, he brought me to his church, which was a nondenomination, the Church of Christ. It took only a few visits till I felt like I was home. This was where I accepted Jesus Christ as my savior and got baptized. I was surrounded by people my age, and it felt right.

However, I drifted away after a couple of years and fell into some dark times. It's not that I lost my faith. It's more that I didn't practice it anymore. I know this happens to a lot of people, and I can only pray they find their way back like I did.

It wasn't until I married and had children that I knew I had to get back to going to church. I wanted my children to be brought up having faith in God. Their father did not like the idea of my bringing the children to what he considered a "holy, rollie" church, so in order to keep peace and with the intent that we would attend together, I decided to convert to the Catholic faith.

I studied with a priest once a week and eventually became Catholic. I brought my children to church every Sunday and, when they were ready, made sure they attended CCD classes where they learned about the Catholic faith. I even became a teacher there.

My son did have a strong faith and became an altar boy. He even wanted his own holy water font in his room. This is the vessel that holds holy water that is blessed by the priest so you can bless yourself when coming into the church.

When I divorced, I continued attending the Catholic church even though I was no longer able to receive Holy Communion. This was one of the many rules the church has and not one I agreed with.

When I moved to Virginia, attending the Catholic church gave me a sense of peace because it was a constant. The mass (service) is the same no matter where you go. It follows the same routine. It was the one unchanging thing in my now-changed world.

When I met my husband, Dan, and moved to Illinois, we tried out different churches, different faiths as he was Lutheran and I was still following the Catholic faith. We found a Catholic church we felt comfortable with and ended up joining it and becoming more involved with the music ministry there.

However, after some time, I didn't feel a peace about it. My friend from work asked me if I had heard of this TV evangelist. I started listening to his sermons and kept wanting to hear more. He spoke about things I never heard in the Catholic church. Even though passages from the Bible were being read in church, when I heard them from this pastor, they started to come alive. I started to get a better understanding of what they meant.

After a work outing, I was driving home and saw a banner that advertised a church that was part of the Lakewood ministry. I knew I had to check it out. It took one visit to convince me that this was where we belonged.

The pastor and his wife lead Lakewood Chapel in Arlington Heights, Illinois. They are associated with the ministry of Lakewood Church in Houston, Texas, and livestream the music every Sunday. The pastor preaches the sermon, which is always mixed with Scripture, real-life application, and humor.

I learned more during my time there than all the years being a part of the Catholic church where the importance was more on following the rules and rituals than on what the Bible was saying.

When I moved back to New Jersey, I found a church through the ministry website.

I started attending regularly with my son. But when my husband was finally able to move to New Jersey, he did not feel that this was the right place for us. I told him to find a new church but gave him the stipulation that it had to be associated with this ministry. He did.

When I let the pastor know that we were leaving this church and going elsewhere, he was very good about it. He told me that I had to follow my husband and was glad he had the opportunity to meet us. This convinced me even more that we were on the right path. Now I'm learning how to let my husband lead.

I had heard that the Lakewood ministry was approached by the movie-theater industry to livestream their church services in theaters nationwide. It was said that the pastor declined because he understood the importance of local churches and did not want to take away from them.

The church my husband chose was led by a Black pastor and his wife, also a pastor. I asked him what made him choose this church. He told me that the messages he listened to reminded him of the style of Pastor Chuck Swindoll, someone he used to listen to all the time. We found out later that there was a reason for this.

I remember the first service we attended. As we were driving into the parking lot, we were directed where to park by a Black man wearing an orange vest. He had a big smile on his face and greeted us with a very warm welcome.

Once we parked, I remember getting out of the car and walking toward the church entrance hearing this wonderful music. This drew me in. I was not used to people singing and clapping, raising their hands, and making a "joyful noise."

My husband was right. We found our new home. At Hope Cathedral, not only are you surrounded by faith-filled people, but you receive messages your spirit needs to hear. I recommend anyone located near Jackson, New Jersey, to come and see for yourself.

When I faced a difficult time in my life, I made sure to continue to attend church and pray. My pastor even called to check on me and make sure I was doing okay. This was during a challenging time in her life as well. When you are experiencing tough times, it's good to know God's got you. He works through His people, and I only hope and pray that I can be there when someone needs me.

Our pastors' vision is of a diversified church, and they have commented several times that when we go to heaven, this is what it will look like. Wow.

Attending this church has opened my eyes. I know there was a reason God brought us here. We found out that our New Jersey pastors and our former pastor and his wife from Illinois knew each other and were friends. I thank God that he led Dan to this church. It's another glimpse into heaven for me.

I have attended many different churches throughout my life. I don't believe, like some churches do, that there is only one true church. Just like people are not created exactly the same, neither are churches, which are made up of people.

Please remember this during your search. If you don't feel comfortable, keep looking, and don't give up. Not everyone is in the same place on their journey. I think that's why God provided so many options.

If you don't already have one, get a Bible. Like churches, there are several options. There are different translations depending on your comfort level. Get one you are comfortable reading. The most important thing is that you read it.

There are people who have several versions so they can compare them in order to get the best understanding of the scriptures. I have both the King James Version that has been in my family for decades and the New International Version, which is much easier to read and understand.

Now that you are a true child of God, seek him daily by praying, reading his Word, and attending church. Spend time with other Christians and in helping others. Use your gifts, and spread the word about our wonderful God. All you need to do is plant the seed, and God will do the rest.

"May the grace of the Lord Jesus Christ, and the love of God, and the fellowship of the Holy Spirit be with you all" (2 Corinthians 13:14).

# ABOUT THE AUTHOR

Janet is a Christian and wants to spread the good news about Jesus Christ to all. She lives in the Jersey Shore area with her husband and son.